Crescendo Publishing Presents

*Instant Insights on...*

RELATIONSHIPS

# Creating a Solid, Lasting Connection with Your Kids

Dr. Vicki Panaccione

small guides. BIG IMPACT.

**Instant Insights On...**

**Creating a Solid, Lasting Connection with Your Kids**
By Dr. Vicki Panaccione

ISBN: 978-1-944177-31-7 (p)
ISBN: 978-1-944177-32-4 (e)

Crescendo Publishing, LLC
300 Carlsbad Village Drive
Ste. 108A, #443
Carlsbad, California 92008-2999

www.CrescendoPublishing.com
GetPublished@CrescendoPublishing.com

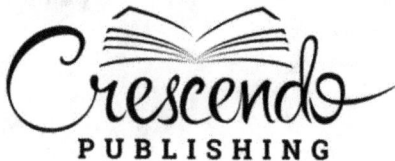

Crescendo
PUBLISHING

# What You'll Learn in this Book

Raising a child is probably the most fulfilling thing you will ever do...and also the most frustrating, nerve-wracking, and gut-wrenching. With all the plans and dreams you have for your children, there are bound to be dashed hopes, unrealized goals, and unmet expectations along the way.

Negative emotions, including anger, disappointment, and frustration may arise within you, and you may find yourself feeling less and less emotionally connected with your children.

Introducing The Connection Cycle™, the revolutionary new parenting program that will help you deal with your feelings and respond to your children in a way that will allow you to create and maintain your emotional connection, from toddlers to teens, and into adulthood.

In this book, you'll get *Instant Insights* on...

- What to do for yourself when you are experiencing negative emotions
- What to do for your children when you are experiencing negative emotions
- How to maintain an extraordinary connection with your children regardless of your emotional state

# A Gift from the Author

To help you implement the strategies mentioned in this *Instant Insights™* book and get the most value from the content, the author has prepared the following bonus gifts we know you will love:

*Free parenting report:*
*Top 10 Tips for Top 10 Parenting Issues*

You can get instant access to these complimentary materials here:

www.TheConnectionCycle.com
Or
www.BetterParentingInstitute.com

# Dedication

This book is dedicated to my amazing son, Alex Panaccione—my inspiration, my student, and my teacher, the one with whom I have the honor of sharing a *CaringConnection*.

I see you ... I get you ... I love you. Now and always.

**Disclaimer:** Presented scenarios are based on a compilation of cases I have had through the years in my child psychology practice. The names and specific details have been changed to protect the confidentiality of all concerned. Any resemblance to actual cases is purely coincidental.

**Please Note:** In order to avoid redundancy, instead of using he/she all the time, I have used "he" in some chapters and "she" in others. However, these tips are gender-neutral, applying equally to girls and boys, and to one child or many children.

# Table of Contents

# *Introduction*
# *The Connection Cycle*™

From the first moment you held your newborn in your arms, you felt an immediate and total bond like no other in the world.  Your heart filled with more love than you thought was possible for this new, sacred being.  That moment was parenting in its purest form.  Your focus was totally on caring for and connecting with your child.

This bond, what I call the *CaringConnection*, is the emotional lifeline between you and your children that is needed to help them develop into the people they are meant to become.  It is through this bond that you teach them that they are loved and valued ... no matter what!

With your newborn, there were no expectations. You did not demand anything from your infant; therefore, there was no disappointment. However, as your children grow and develop, so do your expectations and demands for behavior, performance, and compliance. With these increased demands also come more and more opportunities for you to feel disappointment, anger, and frustration with your children when your expectations are not fulfilled.

The more your negative emotions arise, the more your *CaringConnection* is jeopardized. Yet no matter how old your children are, and regardless of their behavior, they still need to feel loved and valued, and the *CaringConnection* still needs to be protected.

Of course, as a human being, you are bound to have feelings when your children are not living up to your expectations in some way. However, it is the way in which you deal with your feelings— and how you respond to your children—that is the key to maintaining your *CaringConnection*, no matter what you may be dealing with.

The process I have created to help you maintain your *CaringConnection* is called the Connection Cycle.™ It is a process through which you can come full circle, back to the place where you began, feeling connected and in love with your children ... no matter what! The Connection Cycle™ has three steps:

- ***I see you – Recognizing who your children are***
- ***I get you – Understanding where they are coming from***
- ***I love you – Responding to their feelings and needs***

Each chapter in the book presents a scenario from my clinical practice, focusing on an emotional disconnection between parent and child, and an illustration of how the three-step Connection Cycle™ helped reestablish their *CaringConnection.*

When your negative emotions arise, let the Connection Cycle™ guide your responses. Through this process, you too can maintain the *CaringConnection* with your children through all the negative interactions and subsequent emotions that are bound to cross your paths.

After all, maintaining your *CaringConnection* with your children is top priority in my book!

# Staying Connected When Feeling Anger

Of all the emotions families struggle with, anger seems to present the most difficulty. Why is this such a problem?  Well, many of us have been taught that anger is bad and should not be expressed.  As a result, many parents I work with do not know how to express anger or respond to their children's anger in a healthy fashion.

How do you stay connected when angry with your child?

**Scenario:**

A mother and father sat across from their son, wanting me to "fix him."  They had come for counseling because the boy's temper was "out of control." They reported that he had a short fuse, and when angered, he "cusses, yells, throws things, and slams doors." They wanted it to stop. When I asked how they express their own anger in the home, the father grew silent while his cheeks reddened, and his eyes turned downward. Sheepishly he admitted, "I guess I yell, cuss, and slam doors. My wife throws dishes."

**Response:**

The way you express your anger is the model that your children observe. Would it be permissible for your children to behave in the same way? What behaviors are your children learning by observing your expressions of anger? Oftentimes when I explore how parents handle their anger, they admit having the same kind of behaviors as the parents in the above scenario, or other reactions such as hitting, walking out, having a drink, smoking a cigarette, or retreating to their rooms.

When asked which of those coping skills their children can use when angry, they are taken aback. While all of these behaviors are within their "rights" as adults, they certainly would not tolerate any of these kinds of behaviors from their children. In these cases, parents are expecting their children to handle anger better than they are! "Do as I say, not as I do" is ineffective. Children learn what they see and hear.

Is it okay for your children to cuss, throw things, etc.? Certainly not. However, while it is obvious that these behaviors need to be addressed, it is important to acknowledge the underlying feeling that prompted the behavior. When parents just correct the behavior, they miss the fact that their children are angry. While it is important to correct the unacceptable behavior, it is also important to recognize how your children are feeling. Saying, "WOW! You're really mad!" can start a conversation and show your children that you understand.

Here is how these parents learned to use the Connection Cycle™ to reconnect with their son:

***I see you: We acknowledge that you are a human being with feelings.***

In therapy, I asked the parents what they saw when they really looked at their son in this scenario. I helped them to recognize that they were ignoring their son's feelings, and I encouraged them to understand how he felt when angry and what kinds of things he became angry about.

***I get you: We understand that you need to be able to express your feelings.***

The parents also realized that they just kept disciplining their son for his angry behavior without allowing him any expression.

*I love you: We acknowledge that your feelings are very important and you need to have acceptable ways to express them.*

Most importantly, these parents began to identify what would be acceptable ways for their son to express his anger in their home. They also realized the importance of being good role models so that he could learn from their examples.

## Recommendations:

*What to do for yourself:*

When feeling angry with your child, step back, take a deep breath, and relax. If you find yourself reacting, try to remove yourself from the situation long enough to calm down so that you can deal with your child rationally rather than emotionally.

Expressing anger involves self-control and the ability to stay calm. Staying calm means not having a buildup of frustration and stress that you are already carrying around.

Unfortunately, most parents seem to take little time to channel their frustration and anger in healthy ways. They tell me that they do not have time for themselves and therefore do not pursue any outlets to decompress. Parents running on empty are more likely to overreact when their child needs to be disciplined. This is when hurtful things are said, unrealistic consequences ("You're grounded forever") are given, and physical discipline gets out of control.

Take time for yourself. I know it is much easier said than done, but this is extremely important. Finding outlets that work for you will help you maintain your calm when needing to discipline your child. Outlets can include exercise, hobbies, yoga, gardening, reading, music, massage, bubble baths, prayer, relaxation, lunch with friends, scrapbooking, etc. When you take care of yourself, you are in a much better position to effectively parent your child in a calm, self-controlled manner. Then you can address the problem and still maintain your *CaringConnection*.

*What to do for your children:*

There are three major goals in managing your children's anger: accepting the feeling, addressing the inappropriate behavior, and teaching them appropriate ways to channel their anger. It is imperative that we allow our children to express all their feelings and teach acceptable ways to show them.

Most children I talk with think it is not okay to be angry because they get in trouble when mad. Additionally, if they do what their parents do, they get in even more trouble. Children may misbehave when expressing their anger by yelling, hitting, throwing things, etc. As parents, we tell them to use their words and then punish them for saying "mean things" like "I hate you," "You're a mean mommy," or "I wish I didn't have a brother." Their words are expressions of their anger at the moment, usually having nothing to do with how they generally feel when not upset.

Oftentimes, children are told what they are *not* allowed to do, but almost never told what *to* do. If you take a behavior away, try to replace it with an acceptable way to express that anger. Teach them that the feeling is okay, but the behavior is not. You can tell your children, "It's okay to be angry, but not okay to _____. Instead, how about doing _____?"

Children can be taught age-appropriate outlets for handling anger. You might consider physical outlets, such as bop bags or squeeze balls; physical activity, such as shooting hoops or throwing a ball; representation play, such as army men or dinosaurs; relaxation techniques, such as deep breathing or yoga; or expressive play, such as costumes or journals. As their parent, you need to define which behaviors are acceptable in your home while making sure that what you allow is effective for each child. Children need outlets that work for them. Limits: No one gets hurt, and nothing is destroyed.

*Your Instant Insights...*

- You are the role models for how your children learn to handle anger.
- Address behavior from a rational rather than an emotional place.
- Provide suitable outlets for each of your children to use when angry.

# Staying Connected When Feeling Disapproval

You may really disapprove of many things that your children may say or do. When your son comes home and slams the door, your attention is immediately on his behavior. When your daughter says, "You are the meanest mommy in the world," your initial attention is on the hurtful words. Words and actions get our attention. But what are your children really expressing?

How do you stay connected when you disapprove of your child's behavior?

**Scenario:**

Jilly came barreling in the door, threw her backpack down, and ran upstairs. Mother immediately yelled at her to come back down and pick up her backpack. When she did, she blurted out that she didn't need her backpack anymore because she hated her teacher, and she wasn't ever going back to school. To this, her mother responded, "Oh, you don't really mean that. Mrs. Johnson is a very nice teacher. Besides, if you don't go back to school, you'll end up flipping burgers."

**Response:**

This mother immediately disapproved of her daughter's behavior and reacted to it. Her reaction was to yell for the behavior to be corrected. She did not recognize that her daughter was obviously upset about something, nor did she offer any understanding or sympathy. Even when her daughter came back, corrected the behavior, and voiced her anger, the mother missed the opportunity to connect with her. Instead, she negated her daughter's feelings and then used sarcasm rather than concern or validation.

When your children act in a manner with which you disapprove, it is easy to react to the words or behavior. However, a disapproving reaction generally creates a disconnection rather than a connection with them.

I am not saying that the behavior or words should be allowed without correction. For instance, Jilly's thrown backpack needed to be addressed since it is not okay to throw things around. However, if you deal with just the behavior, the backpack may get picked up, but the underlying reason for the behavior never gets identified.

So, what is Jilly's behavior trying to tell her mother? She does not know. All she knows is that Jilly did something she disapproved of. The CaringConnection is strained.

Additionally, sarcasm conveyed only a total lack of understanding. To say she did not mean what she said only dismissed the girl's concerns and disconnected the mother further from her daughter. In this situation, we still do not know why she is so upset! Tuning in to how Jilly is feeling is the only way the mother will be able to actually get to the root of Jilly's problem. Did she get a bad grade? Did the teacher embarrass her in some way? Did someone else get the lead part in the play? Will her mother ever find out?

Here is how this mother learned to use the Connection Cycle™ to reconnect with her daughter:

*I see you: I recognize that you are having a rough day.*

In reviewing the above scenario, this mother was encouraged to focus on her daughter rather than the behavior. Saying, "Jilly, are you okay?" or "Oh, no! What happened?" would have allowed her to connect to the situation in an entirely different manner.

***I get you: I understand that your behavior is a result of an upset feeling.***

She understood that Jilly's behavior had meaning and indicated an underlying feeling of strong discomfort.

***I love you: I honor and care about your feelings.***

She validated that Jilly was struggling with something and cared enough to find out what was going on. When Mom voiced concern about her, rather than the backpack, she found out what had happened that day and how badly Jilly felt about it.

**Recommendations:**

*What to do for yourself:*

When feeling disapproval about your child, step back, take a deep breath, and relax. Your immediate emotional reaction could actually make the situation worse. Generally, when we react from emotion, we overact. When we are calm, we can respond without a heated emotion. Remember the first step in the Connection Cycle™ is "I see you," not "I see your behavior." Tune in to your child. Look beneath the behavior, and try to identify the feeling.

*What to do for your children:*

The way I see it, the problem with communication is a lack of listening—reacting rather than responding. Most parents tend to react to what their children say, rather than respond. What is the difference? When we react, we reflect our own experiences and feelings onto what we have just heard. When we respond, we get in touch with the thoughts and feelings of what is going on with our children.

When our children are trying to tell us something, it is crucial that we respond and not react. When we react, we lose the opportunity to communicate. When we react, we tend to talk; when we talk, it is hard to listen.

Overreacting is a quick way to close down communication. This does not mean you should not share your feelings. There are times we certainly need to voice anger, disapproval, concern, etc. But the way we express it can make all the difference. These kind of responses need to be related calmly enough that your children will listen and not feel degraded. If children fear overreaction or reprisals, they may keep their thoughts, feelings, and experiences to themselves.

When you do not tune in to your children, they will come to believe, "You don't get it!" What is there to "get"? The feeling driving the behavior. Our children's feelings can be very difficult to deal with, particularly when they are expressed through behavior. I believe that behavior is a major way that our children communicate with us, and it is easy to miss the message when the inappropriateness of the behavior needs to be addressed. Commenting, "Wow! You sound really upset. What happened?" would have conveyed to Jilly that her mother was tuning in to her feelings. She then would have stayed connected while finding out what the behavior was all about. Dealing with the feelings first can make the reprimand more effective.

Remember that your children's behavior is sending you a message. Until you explore it, you will not be sure what the message actually is! You can disapprove of the behavior without disapproving of your children. That is the key to maintaining your CaringConnection.

*Your Instant Insights...*

- Respond rather than react.
- Attack the behavior not the child.
- Recognize that behavior is communicating an underlying feeling.

# Staying Connected When Feeling Frustration

In the day-to-day task of raising children, one of the most common feelings I hear from parents is frustration. Children can be incredibly frustrating. They slow you down, they make you late. They do not do what they are told, they do not listen, and they are mean to their siblings. They break objects, spill drinks, make messes, ruin clothing, and spoil occasions.

In the middle of all that frustration, how do you stay connected with your child?

**Scenario:**

It all began with a game of catch. Evan was having the time of his life with his dad. He was joking

21

around, crab-walking to the ball, "throwing" by rolling the ball between his legs, and at one point somersaulting all the way over to his dad and hand-delivering the ball. His dad grew so frustrated with his son's antics that he stormed away, ending the game.

As Evan sat in my office recounting this episode, he commented to me, "I don't think my dad likes me very much."

**Response:**

What went wrong? Simple: the expectations the two had for their game was wildly different. Evan was there to blow off steam and have some fun. His dad was there to teach. Neither was wrong, but when these expectations clashed, the father's frustration boiled over.

Parents commonly experience frustration when expectations are not met. Had Dad stopped to really size up the situation, he might have realized how much Evan wanted to spend time with him, rather than feeling as though Evan was not appreciating his coaching. Instead, they both ended up feeling frustrated and disappointed. Dad expressed his frustration by getting angry and ending the game. Evan ended up feeling unloved.

Here is how the Connection Cycle™ helped this father learn to reconnect with his son:

*I see you: I acknowledge that you are a playful, goofy, fun-loving boy.*

When Dad joined us in my office, I helped him to recognize that his son was not as serious-minded as he was and to dispense with any judgment about that.

*I get you: I accept that you like having fun and want to spend time with your dad.*

Instead of misinterpreting his son's behavior as disrespectful or oppositional, this dad came to understand that being goofy was Evan's way of expressing his excitement and joy at being with his dad.

*I love you: I cherish our playful time together and recognize the need to compromise; there is a time to teach and a time to goof around.*

I encouraged Dad not to take things so seriously so that he could just enjoy his son for who he was. We highlighted compromising when to teach and when to play. Communication helped this father-son duo learn to enjoy being together.

**Recommendations:**

*What to do for yourself:*

When feeling frustrated with your child, step back, take a deep breath, and relax. Try to see where your feeling is coming from. It is not from your child's behavior; it is from the definition you put on your child's behavior. If this father had initially defined the behavior as playful, there would have been no frustration. It was only in defining it as oppositional that frustration arose. Remember that your expectations may be different from your child's. Ask yourself what the ultimate purpose of your interaction really is and if you both have that same purpose.

*What to do for your children:*

Our children will have many interests that they just simply want to enjoy. Sometimes we, as parents, try to improve and promote every stated interest our children have. In doing so, all too often I see children's interests squelched in the name of doing it "right." I have watched creative writing turn into laborious prose with instruction about "using proper grammar." I have watched children's love of reading turn into disdain as they are encouraged to read only "educational" material. And I have watched the Evans of the world lose enthusiasm—and their playful spark.

Evan probably will not become a professional ballplayer. So what? He does not care! He just wanted to have fun with his dad, being the goofy, fun-loving child that he is.

So what happened to just having fun?

When did we get so serious that we forgot how to stop and just be silly and unskilled along with our children? We try so hard to help our children learn and to develop their talents and skills. Sometimes we forget to just stop and enjoy.

My advice is this: Teach children—sure. But in doing so, be careful not to stifle their interest, enthusiasm, and creativity. Allow their interests to expand as they try out different things and discover their own passions. If your piano player just likes to plunk on the keys, let him. He does not have to be a virtuoso. If he wants to learn more, then pursue it. If the avid reader wants to go to the library, take him and let him choose books that are of interest to him, not necessarily what you think he should read—or compromise with a variety of books that you can read together.

If your children are having fun, sit back and relax, or better yet, join in and be in the moment. Enjoy the chance to spend unstructured, noninstructional, undisciplined time with your children. After all, what is the sense of raising children if you cannot enjoy them?

# *Your Instant Insights...*

- Frustration occurs when your expectations are not met.
- Make sure you and your children have similar expectations.
- Take time to have fun with your children!

# Staying Connected When Feeling Disagreement

As parents, we play many roles. The role of teacher is one we take very seriously. It is our job to make sure that our children learn what they need to and to instruct them on the proper way to do things. But sometimes our children want to find their own way. That is when disagreements can set in, and strains in the CaringConnection can occur.

How do you connect with your child when you are in disagreement?

## Scenario 1:

Here is one of my personal recollections:

My brothers and I used to go bowling on Saturday afternoons. I was known for my great curved gutter balls, Michael for his slow but steady rolls between his legs, and Danny for his power ball. Now, Danny had absolutely no bowling technique whatsoever. He did not have a particular place to position himself nor a consistent swing of the ball, and he did not even use the same ball each turn. He would simply grab a ball and throw. His throw was so powerful that the bowling pins trembled in fright. (Personally, I think they threw themselves to the ground in surrender before the ball ever met the pins!) Despite the fact that Danny's power ball netted him strike after strike, our father still kept trying (albeit unsuccessfully) to instruct him on how to "do it right."

## Scenario 2:

Juanita's mother bought a typing program to help her develop speed and accuracy at the keyboard. Her progress was slow. She was having a hard time getting the hang of putting her fingers on the right keys and typing without looking. Now at night, it was a different story. On the computer conversing with her friends, Juanita was a wiz. She had developed a hunt-and-peck system all her own and was able to type faster than most accomplished typists. Yet when her mother noticed her technique, she scolded Juanita by saying, "Do it right or get off the computer."

**Response:**

Both these parents had something to teach their children. They knew the "right" way to accomplish the tasks and wanted to help their children develop those skills. However, sometimes when we find ourselves falling into the parenting trap, we fail to notice that our children have found their own, unique way of being successful.

In Danny's case, his unique style had the desired result—he won every game! Will my brother ever make it on tour as a professional bowler? Absolutely not! But who cares? His technique—or lack thereof—worked for him.

Similarly, in Juanita's case, her hunt-and-peck system enabled her to type extremely quickly, and after all, wasn't that her mother's goal in the first place?

Here is how Juanita's mother learned to use the Connection Cycle™ to maintain her connection:

*I see you: I acknowledge that you are a competent child.*

In session, I encouraged this mother to see her child for the competent individual she was, rather than as someone doing something wrong.

*I get you: I understand that you are capable of figuring out things for yourself.*

Here, her mother recognized that as a competent child, her daughter had the ability to find her own way of doing many things.

*I love you: I appreciate that your way is working well for you.*

And finally, this mother was able to honor her daughter's ability to find her own way of doing things. This did not make the mother wrong; it just validated that different can also be "right."

**Recommendations:**

*What to do for yourself:*

When feeling disagreement with your child, step back, take a deep breath, and relax. Ask yourself if there is a problem with disagreeing. Are you just forcing your way because you want to be "right"? Is your child's way just as viable? As parents, sometimes we are so intent on teaching our children the "right" way that we miss the fact that they have found their own way of accomplishing the very goal we had our sights on.

There is a fine balance between wanting our children to do well versus allowing them freedom to discover their own methods. Sometimes there are both a "right way" and their way. Can't their way also be "right"? I feel that as long as they are meeting the ultimate goal, who are we to say it is wrong?

*What to do for your children:*

When we believe in our children's ability to work it out for themselves, it conveys a sense of trust and competence. One father I worked with was constantly reorganizing his son's backpack because in his words, "It was always a mess." No matter how many times he reorganized it, by the end of the week, it looked like chaos to him once again. I encouraged him to discuss this with his son, who explained that he had his own system and always knew where everything was. This father came to realize that he did not need to find things in his son's backpack—his son did! As long as the system worked for the boy, Dad left well enough alone. (I might add that the father continued to think that his system was "better" but was astute enough to keep his opinion to himself!)

There is an expression that says, "If it's not broken, don't fix it." In each of the above scenarios, that was indeed the case.

Agreeing to disagree can go a long way in maintaining your CaringConnection.

*Your Instant Insights...*

- Agree to disagree.
- Recognize your children as capable, competent individuals.
- Allow your children, whenever possible, to devise their own way.

# Staying Connected When Feeling Disappointment

We all have expectations and hopes for our children, and dreams about how our relationships will be. For example, you may look forward to cheering for your son as the quarterback on the football field. Or you may dream of dressing your daughter in frilly dresses and bows. However, if your son turns out to be uncoordinated and your daughter a tomboy, disappointments can arise. It may then be more difficult to validate your child for who he is because of the disappointment over who he is not. However, if you do not validate your child, he may feel inferior, as though he is disappointing you by not living up to your expectations, or worse yet, he may feel he does not even belong in the family.

How do you stay connected to your child when you are disappointed about who he is (or who he is not)?

**Scenario:**

David loved to play basketball. He played year-round and went to basketball camps in the summer. When he was home, he could be found shooting hoops in the backyard. His sister, Sarah, on the other hand, was a talented cello player who played in two orchestras and was hoping for a college scholarship someday. David's parents brought him to see me because he was being very nasty to his parents and refusing to join the family at Sarah's concerts and competitions. It was not difficult to see the hurt and disappointment in his eyes as he talked to me about his homelife. From his point of view, the world revolved around Sarah. Their parents were always driving her to rehearsals, buying her concert clothes, sitting in her room while she practiced at night, and talking about the rave reviews she was getting from teachers, conductors, and parents in the audiences. There was never time to go to David's games, which they felt to be unimportant because he did not display any real talent and was not going to college on an athletic scholarship. All he kept saying was, "I wish I was like my sister so my parents would love me, too."

## Response:

The disproportionate amount of time these parents were giving one child over the other was, to David, a clear indication that they did not love him. He felt he could not live up to the standards of his sister and was therefore unworthy of love. In a family therapy session, his parents were appalled to hear that he felt like that. They realized that they had become so wrapped up in Sarah's music that they had, in fact, neglected to give David the time and attention he deserved. To these parents, it was never a matter of loving their son; it was a matter of time management and reevaluating priorities.

Here is how the Connection Cycle™ helped these parents learn to reconnect with their son:

*I see you:  We recognize that you have an interest in athletics.*

I encouraged these parents to begin to see their son for the athlete he was, rather than the musician he was not.

*I get you:  We accept that you want to pursue your interest.*

They began to understand that sports were very important to their son, and that this was the way for him to feel accomplished.

*I love you: We value you and will be cheering you on at your games.*

These parents had to come to terms with the fact that even though they knew David was not talented enough to get a college scholarship, they needed to support his passion as much as they supported their daughter's.

## Recommendations:

*What to do for yourself:*

When feeling disappointed by your child, step back, take a deep breath, and relax. Take a look at where your expectations are coming from and why they are so important to you. It is perfectly fine to have your own interests and desires for your child. However, if his interests and abilities do not match your expectations, it is imperative that you keep your disappointment to yourself and support him in his pursuits. Accept him for who he is, and let go of any judgment about who he is not. Otherwise, if he does not receive equal support and acceptance for who he is, he could end up feeling that he is not valuable, lovable, or worthwhile.

*What to do for your children:*

Children need unconditional validation as much as they need unconditional love. That means you need to let your children know that not only are they always loved, but they are also always valued as unique individuals, no matter what they do or do not do.

Our children need to know that they do not need to do anything special in order for us to love and value them. Just as your love helps them learn to love themselves and feel secure and worthwhile, your validation helps them feel recognized for who they are and begin to feel confident, competent, capable, and appreciated for their own specialness.

You need to show your children that they are valued in a variety of ways, and in a variety of situations. You can convey that you value your children for simply existing in your life through love and affirmations, which are the positive messages we tell our children that help develop positive self-esteem, confidence, and validation. There are affirmations we tell our children for no reason at all, unsolicited by behavior, grades, or other accomplishments. We tell them just because they are. Some of my favorites include "I'm so glad to be your mom," "You're awesome!" and "I appreciate you."

Your children also need to know that they are valued for the people they are, and for the qualities and traits that they have. Once we recognize who our children are, we can then show them how we value them for being who they are. If your children have different talents or interests they really want to pursue, find a way to support them in their various activities since these are ways that they express who they are. Supporting them in their endeavors helps maintain your CaringConnection.

*Your Instant Insights...*

- Validate who your children are regardless of whether they meet your expectations.
- Appreciate your children's unique talents, traits, and interests.
- Find ways to share in your children's interests even when they are not your interests.

# Staying Connected When Feeling Dissatisfaction

Children are going to do many things that will not turn out as planned. Their made-up bed is still lumpy despite the numerous demonstrations you have provided. Laundry is still stuffed in the drawers instead of laid out neatly. Dirty dishes make it to the counter, but not into the sink.

There is a great deal of focus in this world on the end result. Either she got an A or not. Either she made a goal or not. Either she won the competition or not.

How do you stay connected with your child when you are dissatisfied with her performance?

## Scenario:

Tami came home with a report card that she was finally proud of. She had brought two Fs up to Ds and the C in band up to an A. She had maintained the other grades, which were two Cs and a B. However, not only were her parents not pleased, they came into the office, furious with their daughter. "Look at these grades! We don't know what to do anymore. She is capable of Bs and Cs, yet she brought home two Ds!"

## Response:

Grades always seem to be a very touchy issue in my office. I certainly understand that, at least for this student, Ds were not ultimately acceptable. However, what about the huge improvements she had made? Bringing two subjects up one letter grade, and another subject up two letter grades was huge! The A was discounted as, "It's only band." The improvements were not viewed as such because they still were not acceptable grades. Tami's parents responded with the same degree of anger to her improvements from Fs to Ds that they would have expressed had the grades remained Fs! Additionally, the fact that Tami was proud of her improvements was totally dismissed! Her pride actually turned to shame and embarrassment.

Here is how these parents learned to use the Connection Cycle™ to maintain their connection:

***I see you: We acknowledge that you are a capable student.***

During our session, I asked these parents to really talk about who their daughter was. I encouraged them to see Tami as capable rather than the failure they were making her out to be.

***I get you: We understand that you are struggling in some subjects.***

These parents also began to recognize that their daughter was actually struggling and not just goofing off or taking her studies lightly.

***I love you: We appreciate your hard work and efforts to improve.***

Finally, they were able to recognize that there were improvements on the report card, and they appreciated their child's efforts. Additionally, they stopped discounting band and acknowledged that a two-letter-grade improvement was commendable.

## Recommendations:

*What to do for yourself:*

When feeling dissatisfied with your child, step back, take a deep breath, and relax. Take a look at your expectations and make sure they are reasonable not only in the long term, but also within a given time period.

Were Tami's parents asking too much of her? Not if she was ultimately capable of being a B/C student. However, expecting a three-letter-grade jump all at once in two subjects? That may not have been as reasonable to expect.

*What to do for your children:*

Appreciating the effort (and not necessarily just the end result) is a great way to respond to your children. Appreciating the process helps your children focus on the whole experience rather than the finished product. Your child colored a picture? Appreciate the detailing, the colors chosen, the time spent. This is much more affirming than simply telling her it is a pretty picture.

Appreciating the progress made even if they did not ultimately hit the mark shows love and recognition for trying. It teaches your children to try. If they have to always succeed/be perfect, they may give up trying. After all, what is the point of improving at all if they cannot reach the goal?

Now, I agree that all children should strive for the grades they are capable of achieving. For some children, Ds are their best. For others like Tami, they are not. I think it is crucial that even when our children have not achieved what they ultimately are capable of achieving, improvements are very important and need to be acknowledged.

Take the opportunity to celebrate improvements, even if the ultimate goal has not been reached. Help your children identify what they did to make the improvements so that those skills and efforts can be utilized to continue improving even more.

Had Tami's parents stopped to explore what she had done to bring her grades up, they may have identified ways to support her through the next grading period.

Asking your children how you can be of help in continuing to make progress is a way of connecting and getting past any disappointment.

*Your Instant Insights...*

- Focus on efforts, not just end results.
- Make sure your expectations are reasonable.
- Honor improvements, not just desired results.

# Staying Connected When Feeling Disillusionment

We all want to raise our children in a happy, nurturing environment where everyone cares about and loves each other. But what if that is not the case?

When your children do not get along, they are not meeting your expectations of what you wanted your family dynamics to look like. Perhaps you want it because that is how you were raised, or perhaps you want what you did not have. In either case, feelings of disillusionment can set in when family members are not getting along.

How do you connect with your children when you are feeling disillusioned with their behavior?

## Scenario:

Totally beside themselves, a mother and father brought their two sons to the office. Their sons fought constantly, and no matter what the parents did, the boys still fought. Even in my office, they glared at each other and had to be seated on opposite sides of the room to keep from kicking each other. "I don't understand it," the mother said. "They're brothers. They're supposed to love each other." The older of the two boys looked at her in anger and simply said, "Why?"

## Response:

It was immediately apparent that not only were the boys angry with each other, they were also extremely angry and resentful toward their parents. In trying to create the family connection they wanted their sons to share, the parents were actually fostering animosity. In fact, not only was this driving the boys farther apart, it was destroying the CaringConnection they shared with their parents.

These parents were trying to force their children to feel and behave in ways their sons did not support. Children are entitled to their own feelings. Just because you want them to feel or behave a certain way does not make it so. Your children did not choose to have siblings; you chose that for them.

Here is how these parents learned to use the Connection Cycle™ to reconnect with their sons:

***I see you: We recognize that you are two unique individuals with your own feelings and needs.***

In therapy, I encouraged the parents to view the boys for who they were—two very distinctly different individuals. They had inadvertently started referring to them as "the boys," as though they were a single entity. Each child wanted to feel special, unique, and separate from the other brother.

***I get you: We understand you both want individuality, privacy, and separate space.***

The parents recognized that as distinct individuals, the boys deserved individual attention, their own belongings (not everything had to be shared), and their own feelings.

***I love you: We validate your feelings and recognize that we cannot make you love each other, or even like each other. We hope that in time you do grow to have a loving relationship, but we recognize we cannot force that on you.***

"I can see how you could feel that way" was a very validating message. This showed their sons that they were understood, even though the parents did not hold those same feelings.

As the parents validated the feelings that the brothers had for each other, some of the animosity actually diminished. Once they were allowed to have a separation of space and possessions, some of the determined rivalry between the brothers decreased. Of course, there were behavioral expectations of courtesy and respect the parents had put in place. The behavior was required, but the feelings were no longer mandatory.

**Recommendations:**

What to do for yourself:

When feeling disillusioned with your child, step back, take a deep breath, and relax. Your expectations may be very different from that of your child. You can view situations only from your perspective unless you check in with how it is for your child. Check to see if your expectations and perspectives may be a source of conflict.

In the case of sibling rivalry, from your perspective, it should not be so difficult for your children to get along. However, from your children's perspectives, they may resent having to share their things, vie for your attention, and deal with comparisons. Oftentimes, parents inadvertently create some of the problem by either taking the side of one child (usually younger) over the other child, or trying to force a relationship onto children who do not want to spend time with each other.

## *What to do for your children:*

1) First of all, be careful not to fuel the fire by inadvertently comparing one child to the other.

2) Do not allow your children to fight in front of you. As long as you feel that serious harm will not occur, walk away and let them work it out. Set firm rules about being physical with each other and enforce them.

3) Be careful not to take sides, and do not reinforce the behavior by paying attention to it. If you must intervene, then everyone should reap the consequences.

4) Be sure to spend individual time with each of your children, giving them your undivided attention.

5) Legitimize their feelings and teach appropriate ways to express them.

6) Assign group projects, and praise cooperation and positive interactions.

7) Do not try to make everything equal. (I actually worked with one family who counted the number of peas on each child's plate!) Children need to learn that they cannot always be the center of attention.

8) Allow each child to have possessions they do not have to share, as well as private space.

*Your Instant Insights...*

- Allow your children to have their feelings.
- Legislate rules for behavior, not feelings.
- Check to see how your perspective may be different from your children's.

# Staying Connected When Feeling Disconnection

We want our children to be able to receive love and to have loving relationships. If you were from a family that was very demonstrative, you probably want to hug and kiss your children as often as possible. If you did not grow up that way, physical displays of affection may be uncomfortable for you.

If you want to hug your child but she is not a hugger, you may feel a detachment that can be very painful. You want to show her how much you love her. However, what if she is not comfortable with the way it is being shown?

How do you stay connected with your child when you are feeling disconnected?

## Scenario:

Bella was a girl with special needs who had been adopted by a very loving family. The more they tried to express their love with physical displays of affection, the more she seemed to rebel. She actually began to run from them and refused to get into bed because she feared they would try to hug her. These well-meaning parents were beside themselves with dismay.

## Response:

By the time these parents came to my office for help, they had already begun to understand Bella's discomfort and reluctantly had stopped trying to hug and kiss her. They were concerned, however, that they had no way to show affection and actually develop a loving connection. We worked hard in therapy sessions to find other ways to convey how much they cared. Well, we discovered that Bella loved water. One of the things she loved best was to put her hands in the sink or the tub and splash around. This became her bedtime ritual, with her parents laughing and splashing in the water along with her. This created its own special bond and allowed them to let her know they loved her in a way she could accept.

Here is how the Connection Cycle™ worked for these parents:

***I see you:  We recognize you to be a lovable child.***

These parents had already seen their daughter for the lovable child she was, despite what seemed to be her behavioral rejection of them.

***I get you:  We understand that you are sensitive about how love is expressed to you.***

They understood that traditional expressions of affection were uncomfortable for their child and recognized her behavior was an expression of that discomfort.

***I love you:  We will love and cherish you in the way that is comfortable for you.***

They honored her by finding and expressing their love and affection in a way that she could comfortably accept.

**Recommendations:**

*What to do for yourself:*

When feeling disconnected from your child, step back, take a deep breath, and relax.  Take a look at why there is a disconnection and how/if you are contributing to the situation in any way.  Try not to take it so personally that you actually create more of a disconnection by withdrawing, rather than trying to find a way to reconnect.

In Bella's case, the parents did not intentionally mean to create a disconnection, but they were actually making it worse by trying to display love in physical ways. Had they taken her behaviors personally, they may have withdrawn from their daughter, feeling that there was no way to be connected. Instead, they recognized how they contributed to her dismay and sought to find other ways to establish a CaringConnection.

*What to do for your children:*

Showing affection is a significant demonstration of love. However, in order for it to be received as affection, it needs to be shown in a way your children will accept it and feel comfortable receiving it.

Be as affectionate as your children will allow. Some children love to be hugged, held, and kissed. Other children are not as comfortable with physical contact and may find hugs too confining and oppressive.

While I am a passionate hugger, I do not assume it is okay to hug anyone else (except my son, of course—he's grown up with my unabashed hugs and still reciprocates as a young adult). In my office, I ask the children I work with if it is okay to give them a hug. Most are happy to comply; a few rather shy away. It is very important not to force children to give affection when they are uncomfortable. They need to learn to trust their internal alarm system and be allowed to avoid either getting or receiving physical affection if it is not desirable to them.

Touching can convey love, comfort, and security. A simple touch can speak volumes without the need to exchange words. A gentle squeeze of the hand conveys, "It'll be okay," and "I'm here for you." A hair tousle says, "I'm proud of you," and "Good job!" Hugs and kisses tell them, "You are safe," and "I love you."

As children become older, they may shy away from some forms of affection that they once enjoyed. It becomes "uncool" to be hugged by your mom in front of your friends, for instance. This is age-appropriate and not a personal rejection. When your children begin to consider the unabashed expressions of love to be embarrassing, there are other, less intrusive ways to show affection. For the child who is a little bit older, or the child who does not like hugs or being held, there are always tickles, clapping games, hand-holding, and back-rubbing.

Preteens may accept a pat on the back or a shoulder massage. Then there are always the grooming techniques: a hair tousle or a finger-combing, straightening the tie or collar, or brushing the hair off the face may do the trick.

For teens, when touching becomes off-limits altogether, you may need to find more creative measures. Try using affectionate gestures, such as winks, thumbs-up, knuckle-bumps, or facial expressions.

Sometimes a private message sent by text, put in a lunch box, or left on the pillow conveys that affectionate connection. Also, the positive affirmations discussed in a previous chapter, such as "I'm so glad to be your mom," "You're awesome!" and "I appreciate you," can speak volumes.

I particularly like the secret codes, such as "SYLA… AAWC" ("See you later, alligator" … "After a while, crocodile!"). My personal favorite between my son and me is "ILYMTYLM" ("I love you more than you love me!").

Many parents play the "I love you more" game. Back and forth you might go, becoming more and more insistent about who has the greatest love. However, my niece came up with the ultimate comeback when her mother tried to one-up her in the love department: "Well, Mom," she declared triumphantly, "I've loved you my whole life!" Touché!

# *Your Instant Insights...*

- Love your children even when they are unlovable.

- Find comfortable ways to show affection to each of your children.

- Words, gestures, and secret signals can also be great displays of affection.

## Staying Connected When Feeling Embarrassment

Back in the day, there was a television show

called Kids Say the Darndest Things with Art Linkletter. The premise of the show was to ask children questions and be entertained by their cute, innocent, and ultimately funny answers. Well, while the show is no longer on the air, you do not have to be a TV show host to know that kids continue to say the darndest things—and they are not always so cute and funny. Oftentimes, parents want to crawl into a hole because of what comes out of their children's mouths.

How do you stay connected with your child when you are feeling embarrassed?

## Scenario 1:

Another personal anecdote:

Years ago, I was preparing to take a maternity leave from the school in which I worked, so I was visiting the various classrooms to tell the students why they would not be seeing me for a while. I went into one third-grade class and asked the students if they knew why I was leaving. One student raised her hand and proudly spelled, "B-A-B-Y!" I told her she was right and asked how she could tell. Another student's hand shot up, and she said, "F-A-T!" Her mother happened to be volunteering in the room and gasped audibly. "Susan, Dr. Vicki isn't fat! Tell her you didn't mean it!" The girl looked puzzled because she had, in fact, said the obvious—and spelled it correctly, no less!

## Scenario 2:

Heidi came into the office needing advice. She had been extremely embarrassed at the grocery store and did not know how to handle it. While waiting in line with her two children, her three-year-old pointed at the portly woman in front of them and said (loudly) to her seven-year-old sister, "Hey, Pammy! Look at that big butt!" Of course, Heidi was mortified, angry, and most of all, clueless about what to do. She did not know if she should have made her daughter apologize on the spot, yell at her, or talk to her later. Instead, she just tried to quiet her daughter down and avert her own gaze.

**Response:**

Children can be brutally honest and not realize the effect of their words. Young children do not have any filters and do not understand embarrassment—they just say what they think! Ultimately, we want to teach our children a sense of discretion—you are just not going to teach that to your preschooler or even your third grader. Susan was taught to always tell the truth. And she did. She had not yet learned the finesse of what not to say, even if it was true. In the minds of both of these children, they told the truth about what they were seeing. They were not at all embarrassed; only their socially conscious mothers bore the brunt of the embarrassment.

Here is how Heidi learned to use the Connection Cycle™ to stay connected with her young one:

*I see you: I realize that you are young, innocent, and naïve.*

What did Heidi see when she really looked at her daughter? She recognized that her little one was innocent and possessed no understanding that what she said was embarrassing.

*I get you: I understand that you were simply telling the truth as you saw it.*

63

She also came to understand that her daughter did not intend to be mean or hurtful and was using her words to tell the truth, just like she had been taught.

*I love you:   I cherish your innocence and recognize that it is not fair to be angry with you about things you do not yet understand.*

She realized how much she loved the pure innocence of her daughter's youth and recognized that there were many things that she still needed to teach her as she becomes ready to understand.

## Recommendations:

*What to do for yourself:*

When feeling embarrassed by your child, step back, take a deep breath, and relax.  Remember that your feelings come from social awareness that your child may not yet possess.  Most of the time, children's embarrassing comments reflect their innocence and immaturity, not an intention to be mean or hurtful.

*What to do for your children:*

We tend to want to take care of the feelings of those around us, rather than realizing the importance of validating/redirecting our children.  Think about this:  Who was the most important person in the above situations?  Whose self-esteem needed to be preserved the most? The stranger's or the child's? Mine or Susan's?

When your children say something that could be considered insulting, ask the other person to understand that you are working on teaching discretion, or help your children reframe it: "She has bad breath" becomes "Would you like to offer her a mint?" or "She smells different than your toothpaste."

You could also try to find nice things to say about people, such as, "He has nice shoes," or "His hair is the same color as Daddy's."

Also, please do not tell your children to apologize because it will not make sense to them, and saying, "She didn't mean it, sorry" is not true. She did mean it because it was the truth! If you try to have them deny it, they may start questioning their own power of observation. These girls called it like they saw it. I was fat! She had a big butt! It is like the Emperor's New Clothes. Only the child was able to tell it like it was—the Emperor had no clothes!

As your children get older, you will want to teach them that some truthful things may be hurtful for others to hear. It is not that children are incorrect when they say things like, "He has no hair," "Her dress is ugly," or "He walks funny." They are speaking the truth as they see it. Sensitize them by putting themselves in the other person's shoes. For instance, ask them, "If you had a big butt, would you like people to talk about it?" or "How would you feel if someone called you fat?" This begins the process of developing empathy and recognition of the feelings of others.

If, however, they do say something that someone could find offensive, encourage them (only if they mean it) to say, "I didn't mean to hurt your feelings."

*Your Instant Insights...*

- Children say the darndest things out of innocence and immaturity.

- Recognize that children will speak their truth without intent to be mean or hurtful.

- Teach children to explore others' feelings by putting themselves in their shoes.

# Wrapping Up

In the beginning, a sacred bond between you and your infant was formed. This emotional bond, the CaringConnection, was created and maintained through your unconditional love and acceptance for your child. With your newborn, there were no expectations. You did not demand anything from your baby, and your baby did not disappoint.

But as your infant begins to grow, your expectations begin to develop, and your child does not always fulfill them. Your unfulfilled expectations lead to negative emotions in the form of anger, disappointment, frustration, etc. In the wake of your negative emotions, your CaringConnection with your children can still be maintained ... if you follow the steps in this book.

You probably noticed a theme in the recommendation section of each chapter. The first sentence always began with: "When feeling _____ about your child, step back, take a deep breath, and relax." It did not matter whether we were talking about disillusionment or disconnection, anger or dissatisfaction. No matter which negative emotion you may be experiencing, the first order of business is to remain or become calm because when emotions go up, rational thinking goes down. That is when the most damage can take place in your CaringConnection. Things get said, reactions are expressed, and actions are taken that can devalue your child and create a great rift in your relationship.

However, by using the three steps of the Connection Cycle,™ your child's self-esteem remains intact. By initially focusing on your child, rather than the behavior, you are much better able to attack the problem, not the child. In this fashion, any situation can calmly be addressed, and your CaringConnection remains intact.

Thank you for becoming the best parent you can be.

*I see you: I recognize that you are a loving, caring parent.*

*I get you: I understand that you want to do the best you can to raise happy, successful children.*

*I love you: I honor you for taking time to read this book and use the Connection Cycle™ to create extraordinary relationships with your children.*

# Acknowledgements

For the past thirty years, I have sat in awe and learned at the feet of children. These are the youngsters whom parents have brought to my office for help, guidance, and advice. These children have been my patients, and also my teachers. They have taught me what they need in order to open up the lines of communication between themselves and their parents. This, in turn, inspired me to create the Connection Cycle™ to help parents create extraordinary relationships with their children.

I would like to express my heartfelt acknowledgement and appreciation to all the parents who have allowed me the privilege of working with their children, as well as to all the children who have honored me by sharing their innermost thoughts and feelings.

*I see you ... I get you ... and I love you all.*

# About the Author

"Dr. Vicki" Panaccione has been called "The World's Expert in Parenting" and "The Oprah Winfrey of Families." She is an internationally recognized child psychologist, speaker, parent coach, media specialist, and best-selling author who has dedicated her 30+ year career working with 100's of children and helping 1000's of parents raise happy, successful kids ... and enjoy the ride! Her passionate seminars have been presented throughout the US, Canada, and most recently, Shanghai, China.

Dr. Vicki is the author of the award-winning books *What Kids Would Tell You...If Only You'd Ask!* and *Your Child's Inner Brilliance (Parent's Guide to Discovery)*, as well as *101 Better Parenting Tips.* Her most recent award-winning collaborative work, *Parents Ask, Experts Answer* can be found on the shelves of Babies R Us.

Dr. Vicki is a much sought-after media expert, frequently quoted in publications such as *The New York Times, Reader's Digest,* National Public Radio (NPR), *People, Parenting* magazine, *Parents* magazine, *Life & Style, Woman's Day, OK,* and *Family Circle*, as well as websites, including *Newsday,*

*Good Housekeeping*, *WebMD*, *Forbes*, *ABC*, *NBC*, *CBS*, *Fox*, *iParenting.com*, and *lovetoknow.com*.

Dr. Vicki is the founder of the Better Parenting Institute in Melbourne, Florida, working exclusively with children, teens, and families. She is also the creator and developer of the revolutionary Connection Cycle,™ helping parents create extraordinary relationships with their children throughout their lives, from toddlers to teens and well into adulthood.

She has been featured internationally on *Heartbeat Radio for Women* with a weekly parenting show and has served as the parenting consultant for parentalwisdom.com, parentingtodayskids.com, and Nickelodeon's website parentsconnect.com. She is the co-creator of Nickelodeon's *The Parent Quiz.*

Her son, Alex, has a PhD in cancer biology from Vanderbilt University. He proudly and fondly remarks, "They call me Dr. Panaccione, while my mom will always be Dr. Vicki."

# Connect with the Author

**Websites:**
www.TheConnectionCycle.com
www.BetterParentingInstitute.com

**Email:**
DrVicki@AskDrVicki.com

**Social media:**
Facebook: www.Facebook.com/AskDrVicki

Twitter: @AskDrVicki

**Address:**
600 East Strawbridge Avenue, Suite 300
Melbourne, FL  32901

# Other Books by this Author

*What Kids Would Tell You...If Only You'd Ask!*

*Your Child's Inner Brilliance*
*(Parent's Guide to Discovery)*

*101 Better Parenting Tips*

*Parents Ask, Experts Answer: Nurturing*

*Happy, Healthy Children*
*(Collaborative work, author Tina Nocera)*

# About Crescendo Publishing

Crescendo Publishing is a boutique-style, concierge VIP publishing company assisting entrepreneurs with writing, publishing, and promoting their books for the purposes of lead-generation and achieving global platform growth, then monetizing it for even more income opportunities.

Check out some of our latest best-selling AuthorPreneurs at http://CrescendoPublishing. com/new-authors/.

**Crescendo**
PUBLISHING

# About the Instant Insights™ Book Series

The *Instant Insights™ Book Series* is a fact-only, short-read, book series written by EXPERTS in very specialized categories. These high-value, high-quality books can be produced in ONLY 6-8 weeks, from concept to launch, in BOTH PRINT & eBOOK Formats!

## This book series is FOR YOU if:

- You are an expert in your niche or area of specialty

- You want to write a book to position yourself as an expert

- You want YOUR OWN book – NOT a chapter in someone else's book

- You want to have a book to give to people when you're speaking at events or simply networking

- You want to have it available quickly

- You don't have the time to invest in writing a 200-page full book

- You don't have a ton of money to invest in the production of a full book – editing, cover design, interior layout, best-seller promotion

- You don't have a ton of time to invest in finding quality contractors for the production of your book – editing, cover design, interior layout, best-seller promotion

For more information on how you can become an *Instant Insights™* author, visit **www.InstantInsightsBooks.com**

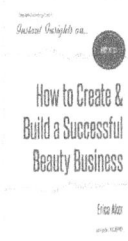

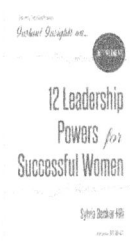

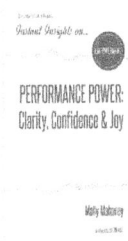

# The Connection Cycle...
# Bringing parents and kids together!

Raising a child is probably the most fulfilling thing you will ever do...and also the most frustrating, nerve-wracking, and gut-wrenching. With all the plans and dreams you have for your children, there are bound to be dashed hopes, unrealized goals, and unmet expectations along the way.

Negative emotions, including anger, disappointment, and frustration may arise within you, and you may find yourself feeling less and less emotionally connected with your children.

Introducing **The Connection Cycle™**, the revolutionary new parenting program that will help you deal with your feelings and respond to your children in a way that will allow you to create and maintain your emotional connection, from toddlers to teens, and into adulthood.

After all, maintaining your emotional connection with your children is top priority in my book!

"Dr. Vicki" Panaccione, founder of the Better Parenting Institute, has been called, "The World's Expert in Parenting." She is an internationally recognized child psychologist, speaker, parent coach, media specialist, and best-selling author who has dedicated her 30+ year career working with 100's of children and helping 1000's of parents raise happy, successful kids...and enjoy the ride! Her revolutionary Connection Cycle™ program helps parents create extraordinary relationships with their children to last a lifetime.

*Crescendo*
PUBLISHING

CrescendoPublishing.com
*cover design by Melody Hunter*

ISBN 9781944177317

90000 >

9 781944 177317

small guides. BIG IMPACT.

# When You Can't Pour From an Empty Glass: CBT Skills for Exhausted Caregivers

Dr. Patricia A. Farrell , author of
How to Be Your Own Therapist